GW01606456

Aerial Photography by Ron Gafni צילומים: רון גפני

ISRAEL FROM ABOVE ישראל בצילומי אוויר

"Israel From Above" takes us on a journey to some of Israel's most well-known locations, holy and secular, east and west, sharing this magnificent refreshing beauty as seen from a unique vantage point.
In order to enhance the connection between the views and their biblical context, quotes from the holy scriptures have been added.

Mount Tabor, Lower Galilee

ישראל בצילומי אוויר
צילומים: רון גפני

Aerial Photography by Ron Gafni

ISRAEL FROM ABOVE

Photography: Ron Gafni
Editing & Production: SkyPics.co.il
Design: Amir Rom
Biblical consulting - Yossi Bechar

Thanks to:
Michael Golan, Reuven G.,
my airborne colleagues.
ArtinClay studio,
Steimatzky
Hot air balloons: Rize.co.il

+972-(0)9-8650068
info@SkyPics.co.il
www.SkyPics.co.il

ישראל בספרי מתנה

ISBN 9789659118038
Made in Israel

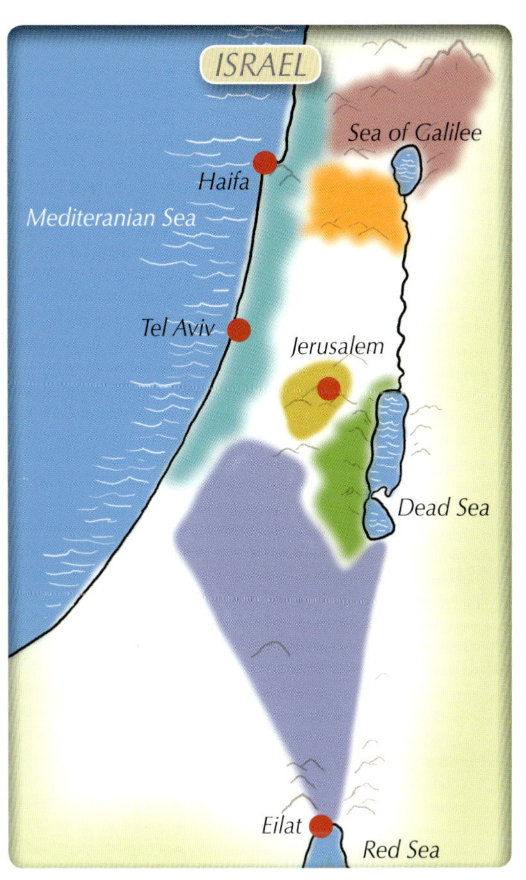

8 Jerusalem

26 Galilee & Golan

42 Dead Sea & Judean Desert

56 Coast Line

74 Northern Valleys

86 Eilat & Southern Deserts

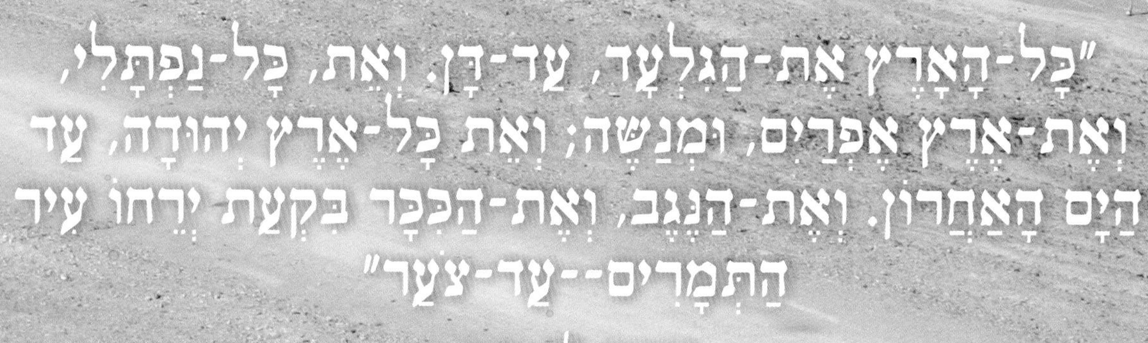

"כָּל-הָאָרֶץ אֶת-הַגִּלְעָד, עַד-דָּן. וְאֵת, כָּל-נַפְתָּלִי,
וְאֶת-אֶרֶץ אֶפְרַיִם, וּמְנַשֶּׁה; וְאֵת כָּל-אֶרֶץ יְהוּדָה, עַד
הַיָּם הָאַחֲרוֹן. וְאֶת-הַנֶּגֶב, וְאֶת-הַכִּכָּר בִּקְעַת יְרֵחוֹ עִיר
הַתְּמָרִים--עַד-צֹעַר"

דברים לד, א-ג

"The whole land—from Gilead to Dan, all of Naphtali, the territory of Ephraim and Manasseh, all the land of Judah as far as the western sea, the Negev and the whole region from the Valley of Jericho, the City of Palms, as far as Zoar"

Deuteronomy 34 1-3

Israel, The Holy Land

The Holy Land, a bridge between the Fertile Crescent of Mesopotamia and the Nile river of Egypt. The land where the eternal book of books was written, birthplace of monotheism. So tiny yet so large. A land of contrasts, a variety of nations, cultures, religions, scenery. But most of all, a land with a unique soul and essence.

Over the centuries known as the land of Canaan, the kingdom of Israel, Judah, Judaea, Palestine, Jund Falastin, the Kingdom of Jerusalem , Palestine, Israel.

Here the prophets gave the world the universal morals of humanity. Every stone is witness to the events of thousands of years. Palaces, fortresses, temples and ruins left by kings, generals, idealists and rebels. A land of historical sites linked to decisive events in the history of mankind.

A land which has drawn explorers and visitors regardless of their religion, nationality, profession or status. These images takes us to an exciting journey through the time tunnel of history as seen from above.

Jerusalem

Old City walls: Jaffa Gate and Tower of David, near by in the center, The Holy Sepulcher Domes at the end of Via Dolorosa

"If I forget you, O Jerusalem, may my right hand forget its skill"

Psalms 137, 5

Jerusalem City and the Judean Desert in the background, the Dead Sea with the Edom mountains on the horizon.

"אִם-אֶשְׁכָּחֵךְ יְרוּשָׁלִָם--תִּשְׁכַּח יְמִינִי" תהלים קלז, ה

"The entire house of Israel brought up the ark of the LORD with shouts and the sound of trumpets, as the ark of the LORD was entering the City of David"

Samuel 2 6,15-16

The Western Wall, the last remnant of the Temple, the most significant site in the world for the Jewish people

"וְדָוִד וְכָל-בֵּית יִשְׂרָאֵל, מַעֲלִים אֶת-אֲרוֹן יְהוָה, בִּתְרוּעָה, וּבְקוֹל שׁוֹפָר וְהָיָה אֲרוֹן יְהוָה, בָּא עִיר דָּוִד" שמואל ב ו, טו- טז

Jewish prayers at the Western wall

Panoramic view of the Old city, The Jewish Quarter in the center and bottom, the Via Dolorosa and Christian Quarter are on the top left where the Muslim Quarter is on the upper right side

The miniature model of the 2nd Temple

David's Harp statue, City of David

"וְהַבַּיִת, אֲשֶׁר בָּנָה הַמֶּלֶךְ שְׁלֹמֹה לַיהוָה--שִׁשִּׁים-אַמָּה אָרְכּוֹ,
וְעֶשְׂרִים רָחְבּוֹ; וּשְׁלֹשִׁים אַמָּה, קוֹמָתוֹ"

מלכים א, פרק ו, ב

"And the house which king Solomon built for the LORD, the length thereof was threescore cubits, and the breadth thereof twenty cubits, and the height thereof thirty cubits"

Kings 1, 6, 1

"So David dwelt in the fort, and called it the city of David. And David built round about from Millo and inward"

2 Samuel 5\9

Israel Museum, A miniature Model of the 2nd Temple within the City of David and on the right, The Shrine of the book.
In 1947 The Dead Sea Scrolls were accidentally found in the caves of Qumran. They are now on display at The Shrine of the Book.

"וַיֵּשֶׁב דָּוִד בַּמְּצֻדָה, וַיִּקְרָא-לָהּ עִיר דָּוִד; וַיִּבֶן דָּוִד סָבִיב, מִן-הַמִּלּוֹא וָבָיְתָה" שמואל ב׳ פרק ה׳ פסוק ט׳

Monument to the Jewish Soldiers and Partisans

Hall of Remembrance

Yad Vashem,
The Holocaust
Martyr's and Heroe's
Remembrance Authority

"And they bring him unto the place Golgotha, which is, being interpreted, The place of a skull"

(Mark 15\22)

The Nativity Church, where Jesus was born in Bethlehem

Inside The Church of the Holy Sepulcher, the Christian Quarter in the Old City of Jerusalem

Russian church of Mary Magdalene, below the Mount of Olives near the Garden of Gethsemane, built by the Russian King Alexander III and dedicated to his mother

Church of All Nations at the Kidron Valley

"And they came to a place which was named Gethsemane: and he saith to his disciples, Sit ye here, while I shall pray"

Mark 14,32

"Jerusalem is built like a city that is closely compacted together"

Psalms 122,3

"יְרוּשָׁלִַם הַבְּנוּיָה כְּעִיר שֶׁחֻבְּרָה־לָּהּ יַחְדָּו:" תהלים קכב, ג' (מתוך שיר המעלות לדוד)

The market in the Old City

The Dome of the Rock ,built in 961 ,was based on the design of the rotunda of the nearby Byzantin Church of the Resurrection.It was probably built on the ruin of the first and second Temples. The dome was first gold leafed in 1962 and redone in 1994

Mishkenot Sha'ananim & Montefiore Windmill, first Jewish settlement outside the Old City

Ein Kerem, A picturesque village dominated by attractive churches commemorating The traditional birthplace of John the Baptist. and the Church of the Visitation built on the traditional site said to be the house of Zacharias and Elizabeth that was visited by St. Mary

Mount Zion, Church and Monastery of the Dormition, the traditional site where the Virgin Mary died, or fell into eternal sleep

Galilee & Golan

Tabgha, the site of the Fish and loaves miracle just below the Mt. of Beatitudes Galilee is often labeled "The Land of the Bible" as it was here that Jesus did most of his preaching and where Jewish scholars produced the rabbinical texts, the Talmud, the Mishnah and the Kabbalah

"And the coast shall go down from Shepham to Riblah, on the east side of Ain; and the border shall descend, and shall reach unto the side of the sea of Chinnereth eastward"

Numbers 34,11

Arbel Cliff above the ancient city of Migdal (Magdala), The Sea of Galilee, with the Golan Heights in the background

"וְיָרַד הַגְּבֻל מִשְּׁפָם הָרִבְלָה, מִקֶּדֶם לָעָיִן; וְיָרַד הַגְּבֻל, וּמָחָה עַל-כֶּתֶף יָם-כִּנֶּרֶת קֵדְמָה"
במדבר לד, יא

Mount of Beatitudes –It is believed that this is where Jesus gave the Sermon on the Mount and where he chose his disciples

"Jordan and his border, even unto the edge of the sea of Chinnereth on the other side Jordan eastward"
Joshua 13,27

"Howbeit there came other boats from Tiberias nigh unto the place where they did eat bread, after that the Lord had given thanks"
John 6,23

Tiberias, The only town on the shores of the Sea of Galilee. Tiberias was established around 20 AD by Herod the Great's son, Herod Antipas. Named after his patron the Roman Emperor Tiberius

"הַיַּרְדֵּן וּגְבֻל עַד קְצֵה יָם כִּנֶּרֶת עֵבֶר הַיַּרְדֵּן מִזְרָחָה..." יהושע יג,כז

Kana, known today as Kafar Kanna, this Arab town, seven km. north-east of Nazareth on the road to Tiberias. Kana, the site of Jesus' first miracle when he changed water into wine

"And he came and dwelt in a city called Nazareth: that it might be fulfilled which was spoken by the prophets, He shall be called a Nazarene"

Matthew 2|23

Nazareth, believed to be the home of Mary and Joseph before the birth of Jesus.
The Basilica of the Annunciation is one of the most holy Christian shrines as it is built on the traditional site of the Annunciation a cave, or perhaps house, where Mary lived

"There the LORD showed him the whole land-from Gilead to Dan, all of Naphtali"

Deuteronomy 34, 1-2

< *Fertile soil of the Jezreel Valley*

The Arbel Cliff above the Sea of Galilee >

"וַיַּרְאֵהוּ יְהוָה אֶת-כָּל-הָאָרֶץ אֶת-הַגִּלְעָד, עַד-דָּן. וְאֵת, כָּל-נַפְתָּלִי" דברים לד, א-ג

This Fish and Loaves Byzantine mosaic, preserved under the Tabgha Church.

"Then cometh Jesus from Galilee to Jordan unto John, to be baptized of him"

(Matthew3|13)

Yardenit, the baptismal site at the Jordan River

Capernaum, Jewish tradition suggests that the name refers to the prophet Nahum, but Capernaum is best known as the home of Jesus when he started his ministry

Amud Canyon, natural structure inside the canyon

The Zavitan Falls

"Therefore with joy shall ye draw water out of the wells of salvation"

Isaiah 12,3

The Meshushim (hexagonal columns) Pool at the Meshushim Stream >

"וּשְׁאַבְתֶּם-מַיִם, בְּשָׂשׂוֹן, מִמַּעַיְנֵי, הַיְשׁוּעָה". ישעיהו י"ב, ג'

Mount Hermon, The country's highest mountain (2766 meters). The snow season is usually late December to early April

The Hula natural resort, National Park since 1998: commemorating the swamp that was dried out by Jewish pioneers during the early 20th century

"And Gilead, and the border of the Geshurites and Maachathites, and all mount Hermon, and all Bashan unto Salcah"

Joshua13,11

Rujm El-Hri, The Israeli Stonehenge at the Golan Heights

"וְהַגִּלְעָד וּגְבוּל הַגְּשׁוּרִי וְהַמַּעֲכָתִי, וְכֹל הַר חֶרְמוֹן וְכָל-הַבָּשָׁן--עַד-סַלְכָה". יהושע י"ג, י"א

"Namely, Bezer in the wilderness, in the plain country, of the Reubenites; and Ramoth in Gilead, of the Gadites; and Golan in Bashan, of the Manassites"

Deuteronomy 4, 43

"אֶת-בֶּצֶר בַּמִּדְבָּר בְּאֶרֶץ
הַמִּישֹׁר, לָרְאוּבֵנִי;
וְאֶת-רָאמֹת בַּגִּלְעָד לַגָּדִי,
וְאֶת-גּוֹלָן בַּבָּשָׁן לַמְנַשִּׁי"

דברים ד, מג

Horse ranch overlooking the sea of Galilee from the Golan slopes

Well known Vineyards, Golan Heights

"And God said, Let the waters bring forth abundantly the moving creature that hath life, and fowl that may fly above the earth in the open firmament of heaven"

Genesis 1,20

Ducks abover the fish ponds, Hula Valley >

"וַיֹּאמֶר אֱלֹהִים--יִשְׁרְצוּ הַמַּיִם, שֶׁרֶץ נֶפֶשׁ חַיָּה; וְעוֹף יְעוֹפֵף עַל-הָאָרֶץ, עַל-פְּנֵי רְקִיעַ הַשָּׁמָיִם" בראשית א, כ

Dead Sea & Judea Desert

Λ *Sunken boat covered with salt*

"Then the LORD rained upon Sodom and upon Gomorrah brimstone and fire from the LORD out of heaven"

Genesis 19,24

Dead Sea, A unique natural phenomenon, the major attraction that is known for its high salt makes it impossible for bathers to sink. The water contain many minerals that ,along with the climate ,provide various health giving properties. (65 km. in length and 18 km. across at its widest point).

Sedom Mountain above the Dead Sea >

"וַיהוָה, הִמְטִיר עַל-סְדֹם וְעַל-עֲמֹרָה--גָּפְרִית וָאֵשׁ: מֵאֵת יְהוָה, מִן-הַשָּׁמָיִם" בראשית יט כד-כו

Masada, combining a spectacular setting with dramatic history. From Josephus Flavius, Roman citizen court historian, whose books have been studied by scholars through the centuries, we learn of the events at Masada , the last spark of revolt.
Built by Herod, Masada was a fortress to 960 zealots. The zealot defenders would win the final victory by not submitting to the Romans

Masada's story of courage and unity which became a legend for the people of Israel

"All these were joined together in the vale of Siddim, which is the salt sea"

Genesis 14,3

Mineral ponds and canals below Sedom Mountain

"כָּל אֵלֶּה חָבְרוּ אֶל עֵמֶק הַשִּׂדִּים הוּא יָם הַמֶּלַח" בראשית יד, ג

Mar Saba Monastery, A Greek Orthodox monastery is on the steep bank of Kidron River in the Judean Desert. It was founded by St Sabas in 482. After an earthquake in 1834 caused considerable damage, the buildings were almost completely reconstructed, hence their impressive appearance today

Qumran, the ancient settlement near the cave where the Dead Sea Scrolls were hidden

Herodion, built by Herod the Great. The palace complex occupies the top of a hill reshaped as part of the construction program about 100 meters around the surrounding area. Built as a chain of fortresses along the Judean Desert

Dead Sea hotels below the Judean Desert ridge. In the canyon behind there is a fresh water pond originating at Ein Bokek >

Dead Sea shore >

Aerial sightseeing along the retreating shores of the Dead Sea >

Water canal at the Dead Sea

"That the waters which came down from above stood and rose up upon an heap very far from the city Adam, that is beside Zaretan: and those that came down toward the sea of the plain, even the salt sea, failed, and were cut off: and the people passed over right against Jericho"

Joshua3,16

"וַיַּעַמְדוּ הַמַּיִם הַיֹּרְדִים מִלְמַעְלָה קָמוּ נֵד-אֶחָד, הַרְחֵק מְאֹד באדם (מֵאָדָם) הָעִיר אֲשֶׁר מִצַּד צָרְתָן, וְהַיֹּרְדִים עַל יָם הָעֲרָבָה יָם-הַמֶּלַח, תַּמּוּ נִכְרָתוּ; וְהָעָם עָבְרוּ, נֶגֶד יְרִיחוֹ"

יהושע ג, טז

St. George's Monastery, Wadi Quelt, was first built in the late 5th century . It was abandoned after the Persians swept through the valley, but it was restored by the crusaders in 1179. Reconstruction began in 1878 and was completed in 1901 by the Greek Orthodox Church

Λ *Mineral mud, found along the banks of the Dead Sea*

Coast Line

Flying over Tel Aviv coast line

"And as for the western border, ye shall even have the great sea for a border: this shall be your west border"

Numbers 34,6

Akko (Acre), one of the world's oldest towns first mentioned in the 19th century BC. In the 13th century BC the town remained Phoenician. After Alexander the Great 's death Akko was taken by the Egyptian Ptolemaists, in 200 BC they lost it to the Syrian Seleucids until the Romans began two centuries of rule. The city is mentioned in the account of Paul's travels

"וְהָיָה לָכֶם הַיָּם הַגָּדוֹל וּגְבוּל; זֶה-יִהְיֶה לָכֶם, גְּבוּל יָם" במדבר לד, ו

Haifa, Israel's third largest city , the country's main port and industrial center

"רְעֵה עַמְּךָ בְשִׁבְטֶךָ, צֹאן נַחֲלָתֶךָ--שֹׁכְנִי לְבָדָד, יַעַר בְּתוֹךְ כַּרְמֶל; יִרְעוּ
בָשָׁן וְגִלְעָד, כִּימֵי עוֹלָם"

מיכה ז, יד

"Feed thy people with thy rod, the flock of thine heritage, which dwell solitarily in the wood, in the midst of Carmel: let them feed in Bashan and Gilead, as in the days of old"

Micah 7,14

Haifa, The Bahai World Center Gardens dominate the area of Mount Carmel directly above the sea port

/\ Caesarea, Roman amphitheatre

Caesarea, Herod the Great established the city in about 22 BC. Caesarea was the Roman capital of Judea for 600 years and was later a Crusader city. Today you can visit the remains , which include the Roman amphitheater, aqueduct and hippodrome and the Crusader city >

Netanya Beach

Caesarea, ancient Roman aqueduct

< Jaffa port and Tel Aviv coast line

"Then I came to them of the captivity at Tel-Abib, that dwelt by the river of Chebar, and I sat where they sat, and remained there astonished among them seven days"

Ezekiel 3,15

"וָאָבוֹא אֶל-הַגּוֹלָה תֵּל אָבִיב הַיֹּשְׁבִים אֶל-נְהַר-כְּבָר, ואשר (וָאֵשֵׁב)--הֵמָּה, יוֹשְׁבִים שָׁם; וָאֵשֵׁב שָׁם שִׁבְעַת יָמִים, מַשְׁמִים בְּתוֹכָם". יחזקאל ג, טו

Sunset over a popular Tel Aviv beach

"But Jonah rose up to flee unto Tarshish from the presence of the LORD, and went down to Joppa; and he found a ship going to Tarshish: so he paid the fare thereof, and went down into it"

Jonah 1,3

Jaffa, archaeologists have dug up remains dating from the 18th century BC, making it one of the oldest cities in the world. This is the place where Hiram landed the Lebanese cedars for Solomon's Temple. It is believed to be the world's oldest working harbor. This is the place where the Old Testament Book of Jonah tells of Jonah's experiences with God and a whale

"ויקם יונה לברח תרשישה. מלפני יהוה; וירד יפו וימצא אניה באה תרשיש, ויתן שכרה וירד בה" יונה א, ג

*Morning trip,
Hadera coast line* >

Extreme competition >

< Modern architecture, high-tech and business centers along the coast line >

NOLTON HOUSE
RSA

Λ *Off Netanya beach*

The Marina of Herzlia >

Northern valleys

Flower fields on the Issaschar Heights

"So Barak went down from mount Tabor, and ten thousand men after him"

Judges 4,14

Mount Tabor, site of the battle between Barak and the army of Jabin, commanded by Sisera. The Church of Transfiguration rests on the top of the mountain

"וַיֵּרֶד בָּרָק מֵהַר תָּבוֹר, וַעֲשֶׂרֶת אֲלָפִים אִישׁ אַחֲרָיו" שופטים ד, יד

Λ Fun & family attractions

Asi River, running through Kibbutz Nir David >

/\ Gilboa mountains above the Beit Shean Valley

"And by the borders of the children of Manasseh, Beth-shean and her towns, Taanach and her towns, Megiddo and her towns, Dor and her towns. In these dwelt the children of Joseph the son of Israel"

1 Chronicles 7,29

Beit Shean ruins, one of the most ancient cities called Scythopolis, the capital of the Decapolis (10 Roman cities in this region), destroyed in the earthquake of 363 AC. >

"וְעַל-יְדֵי בְנֵי-מְנַשֶּׁה, בֵּית-שְׁאָן וּבְנֹתֶיהָ תַּעְנַךְ וּבְנֹתֶיהָ, מְגִדּוֹ וּבְנוֹתֶיהָ, דּוֹר וּבְנוֹתֶיהָ; בְּאֵלֶּה, יָשְׁבוּ, בְּנֵי יוֹסֵף, בֶּן-יִשְׂרָאֵל" דברי הימים א ז, כט

Nahalal village in the Jezreel valley

"And this is the reason of the levy which king Solomon raised; for to build the house of the LORD, and his own house, and Millo, and the wall of Jerusalem, and Hazor, and Megiddo, and Gezer"

1 Kings 9,15

Megiddo is best known as Armageddon, the Biblical symbol for the last battle on earth and was an important city in ancient history. The name Armageddon is derived from the Hebrew name "Har Megiddo". In the 10th century BC, it became one of the kingdom's major cities. Megiddo was known then as the Chariot City where Solomon kept thousands of chariots and horses

"וְזֶה דְבַר-הַמַּס אֲשֶׁר-הֶעֱלָה הַמֶּלֶךְ שְׁלֹמֹה, לִבְנוֹת אֶת-בֵּית יְהוָה וְאֶת-בֵּיתוֹ וְאֶת-הַמִּלּוֹא, וְאֵת, חוֹמַת יְרוּשָׁלִָם; וְאֶת-חָצֹר וְאֶת-מְגִדּוֹ, וְאֶת-גָּזֶר" מלכים א, ט, טו

Migrating birds at Beit Shean Valley, world phenomenon where each year millions of migrating birds cross Israel >

"Moreover the word of the LORD came unto me, saying, Jeremiah, what seest thou? And I said, I see a rod of an almond tree"

Jeremiah 1,11

Almond blossom during "Tu b'Shvat" holiday time >

"וַיְהִי דְבַר-יְהוָה אֵלַי לֵאמֹר, מָה-אַתָּה רֹאֶה יִרְמְיָהוּ; וָאֹמַר, מַקֵּל שָׁקֵד אֲנִי רֹאֶה" ירמיהו א, יא

Fish ponds in the Beit Shean valley

"And he shall be like a tree planted by the rivers of water, that bringeth forth his fruit in his season; his leaf also shall not wither; and whatsoever he doeth shall prosper"

Psalms 1,3

Sachne, a natural pond located below the Gilboa mountains

"וְהָיָה--כְּעֵץ, שָׁתוּל עַל-פַּלְגֵי-מָיִם" תהלים א, ג

Eilat & Southern Deserts

Eilat, Dolphin Reef

"Then went Solomon to Ezion-geber, and to Eloth, at the sea side in the land of Edom"
2 Chronicles 8,17

Eilat is mentioned in the Old Testament as Eloth.It was the port used by King Solomon as his gateway to the Far East trade routes

"אָז הָלַךְ שְׁלֹמֹה לְעֶצְיוֹן-גֶּבֶר וְאֶל-אֵילוֹת, עַל-שְׂפַת הַיָּם--בְּאֶרֶץ אֱדוֹם" דברי הימים ב ח, יז

Special army unit symbols at Katum Mt. in the Ramon Crater

Ramon Crater's magnificently colored soil

"Son of man, set your face against Jerusalem and preach against the sanctuary. Prophesy against the land of Israel

Ezekiel 21, 2

Wheat fields in the dry streams of the Negev Desert >

"בֶּן-אָדָם, שִׂים פָּנֶיךָ דֶּרֶךְ תֵּימָנָה, וְהַטֵּף, אֶל-דָּרוֹם; וְהִנָּבֵא אֶל-יַעַר הַשָּׂדֶה, נֶגֶב" יחזקאל כא,ב

The Negev Desert accounts for almost half of Israel's land area. Although Negev means 'dry land', in our time we are beginning to see it 'blossom as the rose'

"Then your south quarter shall be from the wilderness of Zin along by the coast of Edom, and your south border shall be the outmost coast of the salt sea eastward"

Numbers 34,3

Tzin canyon and the Avdat highlands. On the northern side reside Kibbutz Sde-Boker and the educational institute along with Ben-Gurion's Tomb National Park

"וְהָיָה לָכֶם פְּאַת-נֶגֶב מִמִּדְבַּר-צִן, עַל-יְדֵי אֱדוֹם; וְהָיָה לָכֶם גְּבוּל נֶגֶב, מִקְצֵה יָם-הַמֶּלַח קֵדְמָה" במדבר לד, ג

Ovdat, the ancient Nabatian city, located on the desert trading route, where perfumes and spices were brought out of Arabia, to the Mediterranean ports

And Judah and Israel dwelt safely, every man under his vine and under his fig tree, from Dan even to Beersheba, all the days of Solomon

Kings 1 4,25

Hot Air Balloon over the Negev open fields >

"וַיֵּשֶׁב יְהוּדָה וְיִשְׂרָאֵל לָבֶטַח אִישׁ תַּחַת גַּפְנוֹ וְתַחַת תְּאֵנָתוֹ מִדָּן וְעַד בְּאֵר שָׁבַע כֹּל יְמֵי שְׁלֹמֹה" מלכים א ה,ה

Eilat and colorful surrounding mountains above the Red Sea

Unique geological structures forming the Small Crater

^ Motorcycle random trails generating a "Miro" like picture, Arava near Eilat

V Karate training in the Negev, Kibbutz Kfar Menachem

Anemones (Kalaniot) in blossom at Adoraim stream, Lachish area >

photo: Nadav Hayun

About the photographer:

Ron Gafni (1970, Kibbutz Gaash) works as a professional photographer after more than a decade as a software engineer in Israel's High-Tech Industry. Over his years of flying in different aircrafts, he has accumulated and captured many visible treasures of the land and its people. Gafni shoots mainly aerial photos, as well as urban and scenic landscapes. Some of Gafni's extensive work has been published in the book " Israel From Above" and other albums showing Israel at its best. "Israel From Above" with its newest design is his latest book.